The Perfect Storm
Gicanda (Gigi) Suggs

Copyright © 2017 by Gicanda (Gigi) Suggs All Rights reserved.

This book or any portion thereof may not be reproduced or used in any manner whatsoever without the express written permission of the author. An exception will be made for reviewers, who may quote short excerpts from this work in a review.

ISBN-13: 978-0-692-83696-5

Publishing: Gicanda (Gigi) Suggs
CEO, Unity and Change Entertainment

Dedication

This is dedicated to YOU. Thank you for the love and support. There were times I didn't believe I would ever complete this project. Individuals like you continued to push me towards the finish line. I've met some amazing and caring people on this voyage! I appreciate you so much! Thanks for believing in me.

To my family: "Love recognizes no barriers. It jumps hurdles, leaps fences, penetrates walls to arrive at its destination full of hope."
~ Dr. Maya Angelou
I would do all of these things for you. I Love you All!

Mom, Ri, Bri, I'm glad you are a piece of me. We have all endured quite a journey, together and individually. Thank God for our strength. Words will never express the love I have for you.

Life's situations constantly revolve around you. You have to dig deep and find the light in all circumstances. This task may be harder for some of us, but keep going, and ask God to help you. Quiara, Mommy loves you always! Thanks for being the light in all of my circumstances. You are the greatest gift.

Last, but not least, I commend love for awakening me from a very dark slumber. I did not give up. I'm so glad to have met you. I've learned everything wrong about you and discovered that you are everything right for me. I've seen everything ugly about you, yet you are still beautiful. Love spelled backwards is the beginning of the word evolution. Evolution is to develop gradually. It takes two. I now know what it feels like. God is love, and I am truly blessed

Table of Contents

The Perfect Storm (Intro)	1
The Devil Is Busy	2
This Is For The Brokenhearted	3-6
G. The Hard Way	7-8
Throwback Thursday	9-10
Quiara	11-13
Hardball	14-17
The Gemini	18-19
Mr. Right Over Wrong	20
Human Resources Baby	21-22
Missing Him Is A Crime	23-24
Wonderful Woman	25-27
Are You From Kenya	28-32
Family Fires	33
The Desolate Vacation	34-35
Another Year For Change	36-38
Still Asleep	39
African American Woman (by Uncle Bernard)	40
Every Woman (Caption This)	41
In Love For The First Time	42
I Go In	43-45
Unfamiliar Territory	46
Melroses Are Red	47-49
I Say Thank You	50-51
Stubborn	52-53
Are You Selling Dreams	54
Beauty And The Beast	55-57
Low Pressure	58
Say I'm Free	59-61
Green	62
Shotz Fired	63-65
Born Sinner	66-67
Because Of You	68-69
I Speak Life	70
Iconic	71-72
The Womanizer	73
You Choose	74
Single Bride	75-76
Before We Say I Do	77-78
I Thank You	79-80

God Is Brilliant	81
Sweetest Asset	82-84
Weathering The Storm	85-86
To My Unborn Son	87-88
Just Right	89
Opportunity Missed	90-91
Malerose	92
My Unsocial Network	93
Rage Is Suicide	94-95
The Perfect Storm	96-99
The Aftermath (Outro)	100

What Is A Perfect Storm?

A critical or disastrous situation arising from a rare combination of powerful and unpredictable factors resulting in an event of unusual magnitude

A woman can be a rare combination of powerful and unpredictable factors. I intend to capture every element of me. I present to you the dynamics of my soul…….

The Perfect Storm (Intro)

I've seen hearts destroyed in such magnitude

Was I the blame for any of this?

Do I possess the frenzied behaviors of the butterfly effect?

Am I the spring tide that kept your streams in check

No wonder I've been so petrified

I'm the very clap of thunder from which I hide

My gray clouds reside inside

What you view on my extraterrestrial is terrestrial

Merely by chance I am the avalanche on the mountainous shelf

While my intensions are celestial

I still run from myself

Cyclonic life spins and whirlwinds

My storm surge is powered by low pressure

Always blows through in drastic measures

Down for the ride when the tides subside

My worth is much more than just an expression that describes

But I am a rare combination of circumstances

My beauty is aggregation

I am a phenomenon

Take your chances…..

The Devil Is Busy

The devil is busy

You can tell by the way the man is messed up

The woman is sexed up

And the children disrespect us

Remains in between cohesive teams

Breaks bonds and sabotages dreams

Damages the will to self-heal

Spits venom on the ego ideal

Same reason why your peace can't be still

The annoying light

When you can't doze at night

You count its black sheep

And wonder why you can't sleep

The silent voice that speaks so you assume it's meek

Shape shifted into a sexy physique

Now the devil has your attention

Pay attention, feel the tension

But don't become captive to the apprehension

The rest is in the book, written

This Is for the Broken Hearted

I wish that God would twist the lips of the man or woman who said I love you and didn't mean it

Instead of looking down upon, consider the other mind confined over time

Held in captivity by their commitment to the definition of trust, and not lust

What do they get out of looking into dreamy eyes and telling lies

It's a given that the beginning stage of anything is a round of first impressions

Open hearted but clouded judgments and lessons, cause everything we received in this stage was a blessin'

Chemistry, a positive bond connected the elements that led us in

His hello was the active ingredient in my medicine

And I damn near OD'd

Filling the prescription of love transforms the want to a need

This is for the broken hearted. Turn back now if you don't want to listen

Yes, "you did it to yourself" with no assistance

And the people we thought we were close to seem distant

When they tried to help we showed resistance

So, we kicked them "squares" out of our "circles" forgetting that we ended this

We never stop to realize that we are actually the square

If you look all around and find your whole circle is bare, you are the square

Dare to be different, but you are only a square because you are obsessed with the confusion that is there

He or she will whisper one sweet nothing

Yet we add more weight to it and we try to turn it in to something

But Baby that nothing is just what they mean

You mean no more than the next friend

Fairytale wishing has come to an end

Those dreamy eyes were our weakness

Now we speak less

Pretentious, but it's a reality so we have to move along

Questions dance around your self-decency, but you are strong

They will look at you and wonder how you endured it for so long

Your unlimited talents are limited to the space where only you box them in

And the only space you know is that of your only "friend"

The truth has no illusion, but you are claiming innocence

You defend what you believe is of value.... cognitive dissonance

People will tell you to consider your worth because they never see how you can speak of your growth

You eliminated everyone and everything instead of the one who hurt you the most

Oh, this is only for the broken hearted

My dearly departed, dig deep to the root of the red rose where the love first started

I'm not talking about the one who's always hit on or who's always abused you

I'm talking about the one who encourages you to pray

Who was there when your darkest downpour gave way

Who spoke life to your mind and inserted a promise in your prospect

Remember how hesitant you were to fall for someone else

Now you're at the crossroads of disrespect and neglect

We are rejects

And what did we expect

The more you tried to prove this love you found

The more you discovered that your friend was on the rebound

You were a void they now avoid

And the trust you once committed to is now destroyed

Oh boy

Your friend wasn't there to wipe your tears when you started ballin'

And no one was there to answer though they heard you callin'

And you asked God to fix what he never ordained

That's why I always pray, but I never call him by name

And that is a shame

We're tagged to be "It", but never asked to play the game

Your wounds mean nothing to the Heartbreaker

They don't want to lose you, but can't identify any real need for you

They just want you close enough for when those urges roll through

Now what will you do

You see Broken hearted, this poem is for you

This is for the Broken hearted

G. The Hard Way

Life got more complicated than the algebraic expressions I faced during math time

X factors and minus one and zero denominators undefined

I began to simplify, eliminated Y, and all my like terms combined

Divided only a fraction of the whole problem, because a part of me was still fine

I saw my value was greater than and not equal to the product I was assigned

Cross check, you won't find me next to the alligator mouth with the underline ($\leq$)

Keep up with me so together we can sum up all the tears I've cried

Add that to how long it took to heal the pain inside

Exponential increase for the shame I used to hide

Some number to the tenth power is the formula for the times you've lied

The shaded area in your eyes was my wants and needs multiplied

Round and round we went and that's diameter times pi

Please Excuse My Dear Aunt Sally was the order of operation used to make things okay

To determine the least common denominator, I had to pray

The thrill of the chase plus the lack of faith went astray

Yet, it's the same arithmetic that equals the woman I am today

Once the problem was reduced, the equation I could convey

To get the answer wasn't easy, hence…G the hard way

Throwback Thursday

Ain't no excuse

We livin proof that a youth can come a long way

We keep you fresh ta def in the finest clothes

Cause some of us used to rock sneaks wit holes

Had to sew em closed so no one could see our toes

Whatever we could afford had to be the greatest

You already "got" before they drop the latest

And this is no knock or disrespect to our mom and pop

Together we grew and pushed through to reach the top

We want for you the things we couldn't do

Want you to need for nothing like we are supposed to

I had a damn blast in the streets

No cell phone

Went outside for entertainment you have your arcade at home

When times got hard we had to go and use the neighbors phone

You eat Ramen noodles for a snack

That was our dinner back to back

We had to hustle for our turn

Tried to knock the hustle but got your hand out with no intent to earn

You need to learn why we old school

Thirst for your place in society

Outlive my space and focus on your propriety

That's my only thirst

This is why we work

Now throw that back and call me thirs-tay

It don't mean we slow up

Just took the time allotted to grow up

This is your Throwback Thursday

Quiara

Photography: James R. Hardister III of PhotosbyHollyrock

Fayetteville, NC

Will you ever understand the love you possess?

I wanted to update my status, but I couldn't find the words to express

For over a decade and a half you have been a source of my happiness

Nothing prepares a Mother for Motherhood

I was certainly Blessed

Every stride I've taken with you has been nothing but joy my dear

Sixteen years of smiles and worth whiles

I confessed to wanting a boy, but immediately fell in love with you my child

You enhance my most heightened effort of protection

For my little Choco-latte complexion of perfection

A lifetime connection and prayer that you remain traveling in the right direction

God anticipated grace by inserting peace on your face

Let no circumstances paralyze you with fear

Listen to me as I utter these words

For the Lord will be your confidence

That's three and twenty-six of Proverbs

First John Three and Eighteen

My beloved teen

Let us love…but in truth and action

Your smile is always the latest fashion

Wear it with style as it always fits

You make us so proud and you deserve to hear this…I love you

Hardball (I Am His Rock)

I've been doing this thing way past twenty-four

Now I take my first shot and it's already my second violation

And three on three ain't for Gi

I'm worth a full court

How is it I'm out of sorts

I'm five by five by five times the infinite

Above the minimum of cool points

Been a rebound after a missed attempt

And will assist your positive realities without limits

I steal your agony to make the up and down stop

And to avert your haters shot

I cease that advance step with a block

I am aware that an air ball can easily become an alley oop

A fast break, allowing the forward a clear path to shoot

So I have no choice other than to backdoor cut his or her ass

Or ball fake and bounce pass to my MVP

Who knows exactly where my heart lies

So he will chest pass the ball back to me

This is trust

The Perfect Storm | 15

And it puts you in a position to consider what B.E.E.F. means to you

Cause I'm about to use my **b**alance, **e**yes, **e**lbows, and **f**ollow though

And ain't no benchwarmers gettin in until they've paid their dues

Take the next step, two steps, but not three

If you do make sure you're built to travel this road with Gi

Don't be confused in your position

Transition defense or offense

Choose your lesson

You on the Dee

Best believe I'm taking it to the hole on my next possession

Go ahead and post up Bricklayer

Your team sees your schemes

And grows tired of the player shooting prayers

How many times have you had your hopes rejected?

Stuck your tongue all out for that slam dunk and it was deflected

Here lies your chance to take that secondary break

You gon' layup this time

Or are you dropping the dime

And what if it lands into the hands of a better guard Boo

Now it's mad points in the paint

And none of them points belong to you

Sixth Man

I need a Swing Man wit a mean V-Cut and a solid pivot foot

Knockin' em down from downtown

And got them Rookies shook

I call em Double Nickles

And keep em' wit a loaded gun

I'm not a sideline

So, my coach refuses to sit me on one

I stay in play

Stay in rotation, and bump the cutter

Team winning, and we're about to beat the buzzer

It's only the half, but what we've got is the series ender

I detect what's flagrant and immediately eject my offenders

Because underhanded grannies want to overhand a move that's already been done

But they're over ten

So I'm shooting two

Every time they hit me with one

Correct

I'm not a Double Dribble

I am a Double Bonus Baby

Imagine the adrenaline on the home court and the crowd is going crazy

He looks for me and the look of confidence in him within the stands

And then he finally realizes I am right there in his hands

And it's magic every time he lets me fall

You see, I'm more than just his mate

I am his Rock yall

He looks at me, takes a breath, and makes his wish

We're not playing no average game

This is Hardball…Swish

The Gemini

She's filled with empathy, her overflow in exasperation

Stacked with attainment, or sealed solid with despondency

She's variable

Intimately prodigious and ensues phenomenally

Double the beauty, double the brains

Double the trouble, double the difference

Birthed of twin men, yet indifferent

Intellectually inclined to develop

And although she's the third sign she sees two sides in one

Ruled by the messenger God of the planet closest to the sun

I keep it hot

My disposition shifts, my thoughts are swift, so my discharge sifts

Because in true self defense, fire spits

I'd rather be cool in me and you like the element of air in which this sign is defined

However, I worry

Studies long

No decision is made in a hurry

The level of love combined with my effort is an immeasurable duality

I'm in orbit longer that I need to be

And that's because I see the potential before I embrace the reality

I feel you can make it with originality and determination

I speak to your ego to help you cultivate

Possibilities are endless with a Sovereign mate

There is never a contented finale a Gemini can't create

Gemini is I

Mr. Right Over Wrong

He was a good man, BUT

He wanted to be around me too much

Did corny shit like bought me flowers and such

Oh how now I long for his touch

When I was sick he wanted to be my remedy

Everything he did annoyed the hell out of me

I was used to two timers

corner grinders

And wannabes

Extracurricular activities

The fast life

Stolen cars

Doin a bid with some nigga behind bars

Now I'm mending scars

I thought I was doing "one thing"

My mentality was subpar

If you don't grow you'll continue to sing the same old song

A sad song you've been signing for too long

And you will never choose Mr. Right over Wrong

Human Resources Baby (No Commitment)

"Best Qualified" for the position, but not every job is for me

When I applied, I didn't know that it was only temporary

Nothing was in the announcement. I read it over and over again

I didn't even see it within the verbiage at the end

When asked how many years of experience, I stated, "Over seventeen."

The job required me to be able to handle the issues unforeseen

Give advice on what's beneficial and to possess chemistry

With over fifteen years of experience; there was no need for a degree

Be a team player and commit to your customer's needs

Maintain confidentiality and the applicant succeeds

Administer examinations to certify licensees

Be willing to undergo training where you lack in expertise

"Patience is a Virtue." There will be challenges at a rapid pace

The interview was hands on.

I felt at home in this place

The salary is in abundance, the benefits, potentially vast

The opportunity of a lifetime, and I should not let it pass

I visualized my future. My heart began to throb

I hadn't even started, but I knew I loved this job

On the day of orientation, I was told there has been a change

I could only work part-time, but all of the benefits remain

At some point in the future it may become full-time employment

I, myself, was looking for something more permanent

I handed them my "Veteran" resume, and said, "File this for me.

Please consider me when you're hiring for that future vacancy."

Missing Him Is A Crime

Sincere seduction

Erupted into a pleasurable lust

And we couldn't get enough

Never knew so many emotions of a crush

Built a sexual relationship

No care, no trust

Didn't notice the love coming for us

Running blind

No regard of the warnings and hell's chimes

I call it mine

Yeah it makes my sun shine

Now it's mental

And missing him is a crime

My innocence makes me a victim

I no longer trust me

I fuck up when I pick 'em

Not guilty is my plea

He opened me up and placed a wicked spell upon me

Right outside, we let it ride

Captivated each time our hips would collide

Or the slippery slide of his lips between my thighs

Memories of how a look at me made his mercury rise

Electric convulsions plowing deep

Ecstatic when I reminded him of his Jeep

Thought it was special to get to do it on every one of its seats

Heated my heart

And now it's "No More Sheets"

No longer mine

No longer makes my sun shine

Now it's mental

And missing him is a crime

The verdict is in

And I'm the only one doin the time

Wonderful Woman

She should have her own theme song

She's intellectual

Indescribable

Mystical and magical

Imbibes the weight of the world

Gives birth to all boys and girls

Feminine and her super power compliments masculinity

She hears the cries then flies the skies

Rescues everyone in the vicinity

Bionic, invincible, supersonic senses

You haven't a clue of how prevailing her strength is

Embodied to withstand the force of man

He is strong enough to secure it

But she is built to endure it

Her supremacy is overshadowed but not completely obscured

She fights hand to hand in combat

Immune to battle fatigue

She has a self-healing factor

Willing to take blows for her "Justice League"

The "Bracelets of Submission" clinches life by deflecting destruction

And her beauty alone weakens in strength-like reduction

Submissive although it doesn't reflect inferiority

She's the intellect behind the authority

The absolute majority

She is a wonderful woman

The source of all mankind

Are You From Kenya

Are you from Kenya? His smile was bright and sincere

I looked around and examined my surrounding peers

And I'm certain that the expression on my face illustrated that the question was not clear

Are *you* from Kenya? Yes, you, because I am from Kenya

no accent Although a stereotype, I inquisitively shook my head no

Are you sure? Are you truly telling me no? How so?

Again, I am from Kenya, and you posses a Kenyan glow

You have a Kenyan beauty

And I am astounded by the way your skin speaks to me

The moment I laid eyes on you the backdrop of your environment changed

The American scenery became distorted and my East African landscape arranged

I see you atop of Mount Kenya in the vein of a Queen

And your reflection in the surrounding Indian Ocean from miles away can be seen

Although humid your essence will bless the air with a cool gentle wind

The scent of your perfume will send out a mesmerizing blend

You are not old enough to have known President Kenyatta

And if your name is not Kenya then surely it ought to be

Maybe the vision of your splendor helped lead the country to independency in sixty-three

You have to be from Kenya, because only the presence of the same struggle removes the memory of absolute poverty

We were once rich, but as I stand before you I get a glimpse of my future, and I see glee in uberty

As you stand before me I deem this my destiny

Were you traded in Mombasa by way of Malindi?

Separated from your family by the trick of the enemy?

Do you witness the digging of early graves?

Do you sometimes hear the cries of fellow slaves?

Sure you do

Because the slave mentality still stands before you

Look at our own ways

Overcrowded with hate

Genocidal Holocaust at an extensive rate

Captains of the streets

Ships to Heaven and hell in fleets

We are rebuilding the Amistad

All in the name of God

The Good Ship Jesus

And the lack of knowledge pleases us

Children are Mother and Fatherless

However, we relentlessly conceive while responsibility to educate them is reprieved

Show me the alliance

More Scandals in our own backyard than in Defiance

Because we are defiant

We blame the white man yet place the fate of our future in his hands

Worshipped false Gods

And expected the Alpha and the Omega to spare His rod

Know thyself?

Unite together and know thy wealth

Stop hating on sister Queens

And murdering fellow Kings

Teach our youth to harvest crops planted in our ancestral blood

Let them not forget the triumph of today and honor what was

And I understand we've been religiously divided

But we are God's greatest creations

Over many moons and suns our strength built all of these great nations

I wasn't too surprised when he told me he recognized me

That maybe he'd met more fruits of my descendants in a country I may never see

That my name alone makes me Africa's progeny

The surname of a Queen named Rosalie

My name is Gicanda

You know what?

Yes

I am from Kenya, Botswana, Egypt, Ghana, Nigeria, Tanzania, Rwanda, Uganda……

Yeah. I'm from Kenya

Family Fires

One day we love each other

Subsequently we abominate our own blood

Never considering how blessed we are to know one another

Vital organs compete and compare until their functions are worn

Divided and torn

Neither of them measuring up to the heart

From a family to the blaze of a wild fire we burned

As the future generations of what to come observed and learned

We were left to sort out all that had been concealed

Jealousy spilled like gasoline

And the hunger to outperform, like kerosene

Fire fueled with addiction, violence, ego, and pride

Misery, drama, struggles, and lies

And then my Grandmom died

Still in the middle of that shit

I don't care if she was or was not the flame that sparked it

She was good to me and you

And now there is no more fire for us to tend to

Because no matter what you say about her she always was the glue

The Desolate Vacation

With miles in between I'm better equipped

I'm facing remote thoughts on this isolated trip

The further I drive away the faster life skips

In Solitaire I stand a chance. In Roulette I lost chips

Though I have to part for a while, you are still my kinship

Upon my return we will rejoice, but for now I must dip

This is a real trial and it will test friendship

And I'm willing to let go if there is laxity in your grip

All of the memories we've shared from my mental I will strip

Convert this text into future and now the past we encrypt

I reach for the other seat to get my bag unzipped

When the road is less busy I'll litter the weight of hardship

When I reach my destination I will enjoy this a bit

I will take in the scene of the mountains, moonlit

I'll treat myself to dinner and wear my best outfit

Say my grace and thank God for not allowing me to quit

And for the times he stood by me in situations unfit

And for the spirit in my daughter and our hearts close knit

For redirecting harsh words so that my love could transmit

And this healing is desolate

So that the joy in my future is projected

The Desolate Vacation

Another Year For Change

Last year was sort of mean

Says the suspect who perpetrated identical routines

We all sought that spiritual renewal within messages that are inspirational

And I don't knock it

Our hearts are hardened because our focus is easily breakable

See, at the conclusion of the year before we made deposits of our composites

Our conceptual wholes of madness and we promised to stay on top of it

While every man who deposited that extra change actually profited

Only a man who is about his business could witness

Those who don't put in the work keep crying, "Jesus can you fix this?"

In actuality it wasn't only the year before

Seems like it was the last ten

Spent a year making unchanged decisions and awaited a new year to begin

So we can attempt the same change and screw it up again

I felt like I couldn't wait for some of those years to end

I wasn't living then

I wanted to rush my life by when things didn't meet my eye

We mark the year as a time of new beginnings and fresh starts

Better things, and what future brings, and healed hearts

We think of resolutions and how we are going to do things differently

Some believe that how you bring the year in will define how your year will be

Some of us gain and many of us lose within the time

So we compare those pros and cons to make our gain figures climb

I never did care for resolutions

I struggle to sustain

I just tried something, if I didn't finish, I knew I could try again

We could start anew on any day if we wanted to

As long as it is in God's will, you can do what you want to do

Let's claim that God is okay with it, and the date you set is clear

Do you know what you want to accomplish when you enter the New Year?

It is approaching fast

Use this time to reflect

That's what I'm about to do so that I'm ready for the effect

I need to make sure that my focus is not in vain

I pray for blessings in abundance and I wish you all the same

I'm going to lose some, I know, but I hope only a few

Are you riding with me, or am I losing you too?

Happy Holidays to you. May they bring you a smile

Cherish the moments with whom you love and make your life worth the while

Each day should count

Trust in God without fear

I hope to see you glowing in the Grand New Year

Still Asleep

Many people don't know that we were homeless for a minute

They think the little we've acquired was handed down to us

They don't know all I had to do even when my heart wasn't in it

How the life we lived was inconspicuous

We fought through the masses and benefited from upper classes

We HAD to eat government cheese bitch

Without having to step on my own kind "I rise"

Watching a woman put down another I despise

You killing another brother is not wise because you like to march next to his mother

when a "blue" life takes a "black" one

What a massacre of colors

And I imagine a bond between kings and queens

But the way some of you hate,

You are far from being awake

African American Woman, By Douglas B. Rucker (1993)

I am an African American Woman as bold as the colors of red, black, and green, as deep as the depth of the unreachable ocean floor

I am a beautiful African American Woman for running through my veins is my ancestor's blood that burst through the walls of slavery

I am an intelligent black woman, because from my mind came the pyramids, the first civilization and the greatness in all of the world

And to the dust that made my colored skin I come in all different shades from golden bronze to dark cocoa brown

I am a black sistah who has witnessed the death of my brothers and sisters over a death choice called cocaine and I am here to tell you all that we are better than that because we are doctors we are lawyers we are the best above them all

We are all that

I am an African American Woman as bold as the colors of red, black, and green, as deep as the depth of the unreachable ocean floor

And I am BAD

Every Woman (Caption This)

In Love For The First Time

I've loved in several seasons and was committed from the start

Heated Summer, wet in the Spring, but the chill of the Winter stole my heart

And who knew the climate would create a forecast so clueless

And then the wind blew and who knew the Fall would be so foolish

Leaves the color of black and white lies on withering landscapes

Clouded explanations and the need to translate

Flowers bloomed and we conserved the beauty of daylight

Then time changes and it quickly turns that day dark as night

Yet a cold front came in and froze my body like black ice

I was already on a level, but this blizzard hit me twice

During the storm I remained warm by simply looking in his face

And the only shiver that took over was the fear of what took place

Temperature rises and falls during the flight of romance

And I remember the day I placed my heart in "Your Hands"

So I fight the feeling and realize that "Premium" is prime

Indeed, I am in love for the first time

I Go In

It's all in God's timing

And I believe it regardless

But tell me how much time did God allot selfishness

What about the timing it took to lead up to this

Or the time it took to get in it

Befriend it

Yet in seconds one could end it

Is it really just His timing or did something happen between us

It is not His timing when we meet someone?

Is that not obvious enough

Sometimes it is God's timing, but we have yet to catch up

Life deals a hand

God's physically waiting, yet we are mentally stuck

Spiritually we are lost, but we think it's just bad luck

So, instead of playing one hand we simply give the hell up

Don't even take the time out to sweep the shit up, fuck

We allow the world to walk around it

And believe that God's gonna come and pick it up

Naw son, address it

The Perfect Storm

You think that God does something just for you

And everyone else can access it

Look at me and try to figure out my distinct aspect

I relate to a lot we suppress, but bitch I shine among the best

I grind in God's time

One will never have to guess

I believe in what's mine

And I do it effortless

But do I transgress?

Hell Yes

I can be a motha fuckin mess

God's timing allowed me to take charge of some of the heat flowing through me

But I still need time to work on the emotions controlling me

And I have to admit I don't give a shit about who's patrolling me

As long as Baby girl can see through me the woman she's supposed to be

Here it is I speak words that don't reflect the composure in me

It's just some things on my mind that needs some closure you see

And if I can put it all in some lines and make it rhyme

It's more mature than resulting to things I've done in prime times

Now I'm more complex

Because I am what's next

What I need is articulated

And in God's time I have waited

Unfamiliar Territory

In unfamiliar territory, yet I've been here before

This familiar situation doesn't lack the wisdom anymore

Although my new strength is overwhelming, the battle is not for me

Some things are not for us to challenge, but for God to oversee

I'm glad I've come to know this place

My heart is more than moved

I'm always a work in progress, but I'm proud of how much I've improved

I know that just around the corner the darkness in me will still lurk

But all I can say in reference to that is you have to watch me work

In unfamiliar territory, yet I've been here before

The difference is obviously clear enough, I love you, but I love me more

Melroses Are Red

Photography: Juan Richardson of M.O.I. Photography

Durham, NC

I'm the very color of sexy

That deep spot in the corner pocket

I am the fore play

That never let me go once you've got it

That G Spot but my G ain't for Grafenberg

G is for Good

Paint me honey flavored Baby

Melroses are…

Red like that stop sign

Run it

Because mentally you're mine

My lips and your tip's intertwined

I'm the chocolate over strawberry berry swirls

Poppin' cherries

Sticky candy apple twirls

Melroses are…

Blood rushin

Babe I'd never let you bleed

Grippin the core

Moanin' for more

I yearn for all of your apple seeds

Take a ride on this Little Caboose

After sippin pomegranate juice

I sealed it air tight just for you

Pretty please Daddy knock it loose

Melroses are…

Red light specials every time I'm next to you

I'm visualizing this art on the air

60 Minutes of you in it

Every thrust is deliberate

Grand Premier

Let's show em' how we take it there

You and Melrose

I Say Thank You

Born to live

Passion to give

Thankful

Never unappreciative

I say thank you

Humbled

Learned lessons from having expectations

Break language barriers with actions

Show me

I feed encouragement to next generations

Hoping I have something worth saving

Money is the root

I still salute

Although it will never buy me

God is my witness

My worth is shiftless

It only grows one way

From abuse to excuse

God favored me

He helped me see

Even if I don't show it

I know if you're not good for me

God's love is the only loyalty

For my life

He is the one who fights

I say thank you

Stubborn

I'm stubborn

I'm determined not to change my attitude in spite of a reasonable argument

My position I leave unbent

Inflexible but I have good intent

To everything in which you believe you feel, I'm on the contrary

Willful and strong-willed

I'm obstinate and I will not compromise

My Tombstone shall read "Headstrong" in the days of my demise

This will be my legacy

Difficult and legendary

I am the "I" in my team

I do it all by myself

I appreciate everything you do

But I really don't need any help

Refractive

This is how I live

Reluctant to receive but I will give

Penetrate a layer of my core

I'll give my life to break you so you don't approach me anymore

I'm uncooperative because I don't get it

And my true demeanor is rigid

If what I start gets too close I quit it

But I'm way too stubborn to admit it

Are You Selling Dreams

Excuse me

I couldn't help but overhear

Are you selling dreams?

How much do you charge?

What comes with the cost?

What is the refund policy?

For time and sleep loss?

Rem cycles in rotation

Both phasic and tonic

Penetration, not platonic

Higher hopes in clouded airs

Wicked smiles in your advertisement

Lures to endure your nightmares

Tall tales of exaggerated bait to hook the line

How many good memories will you claim?

Thank God I chose not to let you claim mine

Beauty And The Beast

If I had taken heed a little sooner

I may have missed the end

If I hadn't let it blind me

I may have noticed the trend

Now I see

Now I recognize where the obstacle course was leading me

Life did it on me

Now I rock with destiny

This chick keeps it real

She's walking back to retrieve the rest of me

Said them broken pieces left behind will complete the best of me

Said I need 'em

She told me for too long they've survived off of my delicacy

Allow me to open up

Reveal the inner me

Could you tame such a man-made beast?

Are you patient?

Is your love concrete?

Would you trust that my beauty is skin deep?

Under layers of catastrophe

I don't need you to rescue me

Save yourself if you set me free

Low Pressure

My systolic at eighty six, my diastolic under fifty five

Presently fatigued, but more than ecstatic to be alive

I confess my lack of stress

While my heart beats less

Refuse to narrow my arteries

Due to the side effects

Leading me to infirmaries

Already facing neurosurgery

I used to worry about others

Now it's what's best for me

Growth helped to determine who and what deserves what's left of me

I press

Say I am Free

Wardrobe By: Philly Threads

Say love is me

In overflow

Let go

Released

One captivity

One mystical

One for eternity

Two hearts

Two souls incomplete

Two unique

One escape

Two routes

Two opponents

One bout

One defeat

Two repeats

One mistreat

One retreat

One disagrees

Two flees

One and done

Repeat after me

Say I am free

Green

"I consider myself a crayon. I might not be your favorite color, but one day you'll need me to complete your picture."

The way our spirits align

And our love in bolded designs

It would never matter if the artist drew outside the lines

Life will never paint a perfect picture

But I'm the only shade of green for the grass on the other side

Green like a four-leafed clover

Organic and natural, moreover

The color of adaptation in your environment

A representation of healing

Green is a selfless color

Even the Lord makes you lie in green pastures

I'm the color of GO

Shotz Fired

Photography: James R. Hardister III of PhotosbyHollyrock Photography

Fayetteville, NC

The Perfect Storm

Last subliminal fired at me center mass from the nine

The mission is critical

To the digital pixels of images developed over time

The last of limiting growth due to imaginary lines

Worthy enough to rebuild with bricks for a foundation well defined

The last poem to the last rhyme

The last favor in vast crimes

The last wave of phone chimes

To the last crooked smile alongside mines

The last misunderstanding of a union so sublime

Here's to saying goodbye for the very last time

On burst I send them bullets center mass

Hawkeye

I need for you to feel it

The weapon of choice is the pen

Light like the ruger

Compact yet deadly enough to kill it

They gon charge me for the words I spoke

Guilty Pleasure Still blowing out gun smoke

Doin time for a mind well spent

Pardon what appears to be arrogance

My Shot is magnificent

And there's a difference between cocky and confident

Bust your guns

Born Sinner

This morning's prayer was a little different

Not only did I speak I listened

I was sidetracked by the very words I spoke

My mind began to travel as a lump swelled in my throat

Hard to swallow

Tears followed

I realized my focus was gone and tried to retrieve it

And the prayer I just asked the Lord for I cried to believe it

The anticipation of what the future has in store is worth achieving

The gore caused by the struggle inside is worth some grieving

See it only hurts until it doesn't hurt anymore and God is easing

But am I pleasing Him

I'm still spittin but I'm listenin

I don't want to take anything out of context

Now I'm a mess but I know what's next

Just as sure as I'm typing this text

I know I have to face something even more complex

I'm talking to God and my feeling is odd

I love the Lord because he heard when I cried

I trust him more and more because I know deep inside

I would have never made it this far on my pride

Born sinner

Destined winner

New life beginner

Because Of You

A friend reached out to me about my latest poetry

He said Gi why are you rationing it

I don't give a damn about what's changing in you

Keep putting your passion in it

I said I don't want to seem harsh or negative

So I was trying to relax

In a brief silence I heard the frustration and wanted to take those words back

He asked who in the heck can identify negativity in one who's stating the facts

I said apparently not everything is worth mentioning

I was offending people

Or perhaps

Or perhaps I am just Gi

And I deal with obstinate cats

Who can idolize the total stranger because that's where their history lacks

Clean slate on the surface

Internal revelations about the past

Memories on the run

Mentalities struck

No endurance to make it last

Nonetheless

With you I smell sweet success

You don't give up on me

I digress

I Speak Life

"Seven days without God makes one weak."

Have you given God those seven days?

Wasted tears fall

Tears not falling at all

Clouds barricade the sky

Darkness will empower the sun rays

Watch who and what you allow in

Trust your vital organ

Without it, a situation is dead

Give God trust

Have faith that with Him you will never be misled

Every breath you breathe is love

I inhale deep to fill my capacity

I know there is a joy in store for me

To believe that God has not a plan is blasphemy

Yes, I am weak

But it is life I speak

Iconic

Find serenity in the direction of your reflection

The fondest blessings are in your possession

Walk a walk no man or woman can appease

Think a thought so strong your entire being will take the lead

Talk a talk so empowering that your character is understood

That even in your absence they know your spirit is good

As they should

Live a life so blissful they beg for it

Then share it with em

Not to boast or brag

But to let them know you'd spare it

To embrace the joy of making more

This time create it bigger than ever before

Never doubt such a remarkable you

See that there is a divinity inside

You'll never know it until the image is clearer

So don't forget to love that beautiful likeness in the mirror

Be Iconic

Like a God

Wardrobe By: ICONIC

The Womanizer

God is my witness

she no longer wanted this

Womanizers are manipulative

because of pain she is combative

but that pain she should out live

She looked up to him

her biggest mistake was trusting again

but he was consistent

persistent

showed her love was the reason for his existence

She didn't want to love

he pulled her in until she did

for years her feelings she hid

she gave in and he slid

did the ultimate

evaded and lied in subsequent

looked right in her eyes as she cried

as he slowly said goodbye she died

he quickly found another poor soul to womanize

You Choose

Everything in life is a result of choice

Don't plan

Because that's where you stand to lose your voice

Don't push and do not insist

It does not belong to you if it resists

You can only place claim if it's consistent

You have yourself to blame when you don't listen

You can't foresee the path for you but you can choose

You can choose who to love on day and who to lose

Single Bride

I prayed that God would yoke me, equally

So that I could set pain free

Said Father let him love me as he loves the church

Not only because you said so but because I need someone to grow with me

spiritually

My spirit desires to be fed

My passion led

By a partner as willing to commit as I'm willing to submit

God said do not be deceived

What fellowship has light with darkness?

Then I showed Him my soul

And even God cried

For deep within my darkness God saw light and revealed it to me

He said that is the place you want your soul mate to be

Before We Say I Do

Hey Beautiful. Take heed and know where you really stand in his life

Before planning your future of being his wife

Does he make you know you are the only one

Or does he explore other options and say he's having fun

Does he publicly downplay your relation and privately confirm what you feel

If that's the case you should never question if what you have is real

Maybe he is indecisive about seeing you in his vision

Just know that indecisiveness is a decision

Maybe you believe meeting him was the best and you now believe in fate

So you tolerate the nonsense and miserably wait

Can you feel the love off in the distance

Or does your heart go cold in that very instance

Hey Beautiful. There is a lack of respect these days

Less faithfulness, less commitment, and a heap of wicked ways

Now we are no angels. We give our all and he doesn't measure up

And we blame him as if he would give the pleasure up

So that lack of respect begins from within

Hold yourself responsible for assuming that he is more than a friend

He would shower you with happiness when the road is rough

If his heart had been captured, he could never get enough

He may forget your first kiss, your first date, your first nights stay

Your anniversary, etc., but he'd remember you each day

Your tears would be filled with joy and your years together would make God smile

Wait happily for the man worth the while

Hey Beautiful. Take heed and know where you really stand in his life

Before planning your future of being his wife

I Thank You

Moment of truth

Too often I think of you

Call me crazy because my heart's been in love with the same man for some time now, years in fact

It's one of those things we hear about as youths

Something will surface and make you question your pact

You know, like how powerful is your foundation attached

I chose to wait

Enduring as equal tears as hope for mutual solidity

That may never ever come

Longing for what seems to be the sun and stars to become one

I no longer care for the dark magic

At every abracadabra, my heart is getting stabbed at

And now you are on my mind

But there is not one thing I would do

This is the life that I led myself to

It comes naturally with you

Most importantly, you love to see me smile

You are my moment of truth

And for what it's worth, I thank you

God Is Brilliant

Spend enough time in the eye of a storm

You'll assume the storm is over

Peace is still

In the calm God will empower you

It indeed shall be his will

Bring the rain and pain

He has already built you with resilience

Blow the force of a hurricane

His love is selfless

And my God is BRILLIANT...

Photography: Juan Richardson of M.O.I. Photography

Durham, NC

The Sweetest Asset

Before "The Fall" her nakedness did not matter

God took his time

Smiling at the many shapes and ways to format her

Molded from the finest of character

The most beautiful

She was the fifth element

The purest and supreme spiritual being

Decreeing that each curve He sculpted was worth seeing

Yahweh went to work while man slept

He would not need man's help, as my God is adept

Beneath layers of exquisiteness she was impregnated with wisdom

A "helpmate" suitable to answer all of the things that quizzed him

This body embodies the heart of intimacy

Built to survive the afflictions of intricacies

Elohim wrapped in "one" flesh a Goddess

It was unnecessary to be clothed in dresses and bodices

For whatever look God gave you, you meant no less

We desire to change our "out" look

Just consider the commitment the Creator undertook

Queen you are perfection from the crown to the toe

Lest you ever forget

Before "The Fall" she was the SWEETEST ASSET

Weathering The Storm

What's about to happen is nothing short of miraculous

I put a time frame on the pain

A limit to the shame

The end is near and there is no lack thereof

I promised to give the best of me

Didn't give a damn who thought any less of me

I pray more, give more, love more

What I thought would exhaust me fueled my core

I'm finally ready

Plunging into the next chapter

Had to hit rock bottom to come up

Had to see the before in order to get after

How is it she gets to live this life

Because even today she's more than willing to sacrifice

I give in

Willing to lose my loved ones

Willing to lose my friends

Suffering could turn into tradition

If we are always on the left one of us are out of position

I want to make it right

No need to fight

I'll be the first in flight

Mrs. Right

Teach me how to cope and watch me learn

Show me heart's desire and I'll watch it burn

This is goodbye and hello

I'm down for taking time off

Put the misunderstanding on furlough

Sequestration

To seek less frustration

I take possession of heartfelt blessings

Nothing's short of miraculous

Nothing more nothing less

To My Unborn Son

You tiptoed into my world unnoticed

Silent

Leaving imprints of tiny footprints

Within my broken heart

For your life I've always prayed

Often, alone, I imagine what you would have looked like

Mommy only wishes you could have stayed

She, too, is her own friend, because she laid on that table alone

Private moments and prayer requests

Sincere condolences over the phone

And alone she pressed

She smiled because she vowed to get that loss off of her chest

Life was created in the absence of bane

On deaf ears her cries were estranged

And God was the only one who understood the pain

Then she realized the cries were not her cries

She told her baby goodbye

As thousands of infant tears began to pour from her eyes

Microscopic remains and bloodstained imageries

And she visualizes that

Only God can heal her spiritually

From such a lasting impact

Just Right

I saw tears in his smile

The damage to his heart

I heard the cry for a new beginning

I temporarily mended an open wound

And later discovered how it was self inflicted

Age and maturity was never in tune

But the pain was addictive

I loved him just right

Opportunity Missed

Cordial conversations lead to a present mind

Our thoughts fueling words and igniting flames at the same time

"Us" is clearly fraternal with an identical twist

Like is an understatement, though we agree that it fits

Determine what is what, and we'll both get sucked in

Together we face our struggles and are determined to win

Has-beens and bygones shared between lifetime friends

It's out of concern we ask of answers and all the while it's so sincere

Still the wonder of possibilities is just what draws us near

Being true to one another and the laughter keeps us straight

Everyday is anticipated, and each moment is worth the wait

Another beginning for new feeling is a great rush

Never really thinking about the true concept of us

Openly we state emotion

Plainly causing commotion

Partaking in the act of brainstorming devotion

Once we make moves, what will become

Regret is beyond the core of which we both come from

Time is of the essence, and the visions are clear

Uniting what was lost in a new atmosphere

Notions to run away is every reason to stay

In light of something new, yet real enough to stray

The concept of never being is long gone

Youthful mentalities can sense an adulthood that's strong

Magic is the answer to the one that was in need

Instinct is the reaction to the manual speed

Sharing lifestyles similar to code defenders

Sparking a light in something similar

Evolving around a situation that seems so divine

Dare you read the first letters of each line

Male Rose

Imagine the calm of the ocean

Even the mesmerizing movement of the tides

Close your eyes as the birds serenade you with music

Embrace the freedom they possess in the skies

Watch the clouds blow in strange and peculiar

Feel the warmth of the sun as it fades away

Notice that everything around seems dim and cold

In just a moment all is lost of the day

Now the clouds often symbolize a storm

But there is much more greatness due to the rain

Deep down in the darkness of the soil

Is a root being healed of constant pain

You are my ocean, you are my bird, you are my sun

You are my rain, you are my smile, you are the ONE

Look beyond what seems to be the worst

Be patient as I try to understand

The true beauty in such a rugged flower

Who has blossomed into who my heart demands

My Unsocial Network

Don't attempt to be Joe Familiar and "request" to analyze me

Or "search" me out of hatred and "share" what you see

Don't anticipate my next "check in" and show up at where I may be

Or request to "tag" a photo when the only one in it is me

Don't befriend all of my neighbors just to be in the vicinity

Or try to duplicate my moves and compare femininity

Don't slip up and fall on the ice I place before thee

You're used to skating by undetected, but you are no Gretzky

Don't send "messages" with fake content in attempt to provoke me

You want a reaction? Yahoo Sports and ESPN can help you create a fantasy

You can't help but "like" the feeling you get when you recognize reality

I'm not your "status". You can't "update" what's already great in me

There's a reason I maintain composure when faced with adversity

It is a waste of time when you are not worth a "comment" to me

I love you, but we are not "friends" and I am not your "FB"

Plus you "deactivated" any chance of "logging in" to me

Rage Is Suicide

Over three hundred and fifty-seven ways

My hesitation is imperative

Relinquish the life that I live?

Tyrannical results are what it's adequate to

If you send for me, do I come for you?

Stroke the backbone

Provoke an act so wretched

Rage is suicide

Because even I can catch it

Photography: James R. Hardister III of PhotosbyHollyrock Photography

Fayetteville, NC

The Perfect Storm

I've seen hearts destroyed in such magnitude

Was I the blame for any of this?

Do I possess the frenzied behaviors of the butterfly effect?

Am I the spring tide that kept your streams in check

No wonder I've been so petrified

I'm the very clap of thunder from which I hide

My gray clouds reside inside

What you view on my extraterrestrial is terrestrial

Merely by chance I am the avalanche on the mountainous shelf

While my intensions are celestial

I still run from myself

Cyclonic life spins and whirlwinds

My storm surge is powered by low pressure

Always blows through in drastic measures

Down for the ride when the tides subside

My worth is much more than just an expression that describes

But I am a rare combination of circumstances

My beauty is aggregation

I am a phenomenon

Take your chances

The Perfect Storm

Every element of me is a synergy

Ominous

Be prepared for me

They call me chaos

I'm predicted

Falsely depicted

No man proved strong enough to survive

They get caught up in the calm of my eye

But no one will commit to a category five

I'm heavy precipitation

But I reign supreme

I am a queen

I rise

Mentality more sophisticated than what's between my thighs

Tsunami flow from the oceans

But I produce high winds

Dynamically true

I am everything good for you

I'm not perfect

Yet I'm perfect

And certainly a storm worth living through

The Aftermath (Outro)

He let her go and she still held on

Her grace could see far beyond what he ever intended to look for

Looking into his eyes in disbelief

She watched the memories disappear

He remembered her million dollar mocha skin

Laughter

Even the promise of ever after

He reached for her

Only this time she let go

The fear of falling to the end now confronted

God had a mate for her

And after falling for so many years

She finally fell right into his arms.....

Reciprocal sunset

They say time will tell

And it's been many moons

I'll be the sunrise

In the eyes on the horizon

Look for me in the Aftermath….....

The Aftermath
COMING SOON

Contact Gigi

 www.unityandchangeent.com

 unityandchangeent@gmail.com

Unity and Change Entertainment

Gi's Spot

Unity and Change Entertainment

unityandchange1

www.ingramcontent.com/pod-product-compliance
Lightning Source LLC
Chambersburg PA
CBHW042315150426
43201CB00001B/6